BUDDY

THE SPECIAL CHESTNUT HORSE

Written by Gillian Shepherd
Illustrated by Amy Curran

DEDICATION

To Buddy
and all the horses in my life
who have taken me into their
lives and taught me so much about
patience and trust and
the importance of standing up for
what you believe in.

Buddy the Special Chestnut Horse
ISBN: 978-0-6482393-7-6

A Tales of Tails Early Reader

Published in Australia by
PINK COFFEE PUBLISHING
PO Box 483, Oberon NSW 2787
www.pinkcoffeepublishing.com

Text and Illustrations Copyright Amy Curran 2018
All Rights Reserved

National Library of Australia Cataloguing-in-Publication entry information can be found at www.nla.gov.au

CONTENTS

Chaper One	5
Chapter Two	9
Chapter Three	13
Chapter Four	17
Chapter Five	21
Chapter Six	27
Chapter Seven	35
Chapter Eight	43

CHAPTER ONE

Buddy was a beautiful chestnut horse. He had a sister who was older than him called Nomi, and she was also very beautiful. Both of them had a very unusual white marking on their faces, called a blaze, shaped like the number 1.

When Buddy was born, his mother and father looked at the blaze that was just like Nomi's and knew he was special. They told him he and Nomi were special horses, and that they could do anything they put their minds to.

They could run fast, they could leap high and gracefully, and they had big hearts that could help many people when they grew up.

Nomi was so courageous and brave, but Buddy was a little scared of anything that was new.

Nomi was always first to investigate new things, but Buddy was shy and a little afraid. It didn't matter though, because their mother and father were always close by.

Buddy and Nomi lived with a lady called Ginny, who loved them very much. She watched them grow up and cared for them daily and would always tell them how special they were.

One day Nomi left the farm to go to school. She was to be trained to take a rider so she could show the world how beautiful and talented she was.

Buddy was so sad, as he loved his sister, but Mother and Father told him that Nomi would be treated well and be happy in her new life.

CHAPTER TWO

When Nomi arrived at her school, they didn't understand her. They were very rough with her, as they thought she was naughty. They did not see that she was clever; instead, they just thought she was bad.

Nomi tried and tried to show them that she could do lots of things, leaping high and gracefully. But the trainer just trained her harder and harder. Nomi got sad and angry. All the other horses at the school told her to be like them and do everything the trainer wanted.

But Nomi was brave, and just stamped her hoof and snorted. Her mother and father had taught her to stand up for herself.

She felt so hopeless and lonely. No one understood her.

The trainer tried all the things he knew, but he did not know how to train a horse like Nomi, so he sent her back home. He told Ginny that Nomi was a naughty horse and would never learn to take a rider.

Ginny was angry with the trainer and sad that she had chosen the wrong school for Nomi, who was now very angry with everyone. Even with Buddy.

Buddy was very sad and frightened of his sister now, who was always in a bad mood and no longer wanted to play with him.

CHAPTER THREE

When it became his turn to go to school, Buddy was very scared, as Nomi had told him how horrible it was. Buddy had become scared of all strange men, and whenever a new man came to see the horses, he would hide and not come out until they were gone.

The day arrived when Ginny took him to school. He was so scared that he trembled all the way in the horse trailer. When they arrived at the school, Buddy looked around fearfully for the horrible man that would be his trainer.

To his surprise it was a lady. Her name was Kate and she looked nice. She rubbed and scratched him all over while Ginny was there. Buddy was hopeful that this would be a good school, not like Nomi's, and he would be able to show his special talents.

Kate and Buddy waved goodbye to Ginny, and then Kate turned to Buddy and said, "You are beautiful and tall and strong and will take a big rider. I have so many horses to work with. I will give you to my brother to train."

Oh no, thought Buddy, a man!

I don't want to be trained by a man.

I want you!

He tried to tell Kate his thoughts by licking her arm and rubbing his head against her side, but she pushed him away. He backed away and pulled the rope out of her hands, and in a panic he ran and hid.

It took Kate and her brother Bill a long time to corner and catch him. He was still so frightened after they caught him that he stood in the corner of the stable and would not eat his dinner.

CHAPTER FOUR

The next day, Bill came to start training Buddy. Buddy was very scared, but Bill seemed to be a gentle and patient man. He took the time to explain to Buddy all the things he needed to learn to take a rider and be as beautiful as he could be.

Day by day Buddy grew a little braver, but it was slow progress, and Kate told Bill he was taking too long. They argued about Buddy's training. Buddy was sad that Kate and Bill were not happy with him; he was trying so hard! But anything new was still scary to him, and he took a longer time than the other horses to understand things.

Ginny came and took him home, and Kate told her that he was a scared horse and it would take a special rider to bring him out of his shell.

Ginny was sad. Now she had two horses that would be hard to find forever homes for: Nomi who was angry and Buddy who was scared.

Many people came to see Nomi and Buddy to try them, but most of them didn't want to take them home. The few people that did want to take them, Ginny could see that Nomi and Buddy didn't like them.

One day a lady called Janey came, and Nomi pricked up her ears as soon as she saw her and said, "That's the owner for me." She just felt it in her heart. She trotted over to the fence and sniffed and licked Janey from head to toe, and Ginny was very surprised.

Janey took Nomi home, and they were both very happy. Buddy was very happy for Nomi and longed for an owner like Janey, who would understand him, and he could be happy and not scared of everything.

Would Buddy ever find such a special person?

CHAPTER FIVE

Ginny loved her horses so much that she decided she would organise a lady to come and give them all a massage.

Buddy and his father were tied up in the yard together when Jill the bodyworker arrived. Ginny introduced Jill to Buddy's father so she could get started on the massage.

Jill saw Buddy and asked Ginny, "Who is this beautiful horse?"

Ginny said, "That is Buddy. He is waiting for a new owner to try him, but if he is not sold today, could you please give him a special massage too?"

"Yes, I have enough time today to work on him. He looks sad and worried, but he is so beautiful he should be happy," said Jill.

Buddy heard this and edged closer to Jill. Could this lady really see how scared and unhappy he was?

Jill walked over to Buddy and held out her hand. He sniffed it, and he liked the way she smelt. He licked her hand and loved the taste.

She whispered to him, "You poor boy, I can see how scared you are and how special and sensitive you are. I wish I could take you home, but I am so small and you are so tall, and I cannot afford to buy you. I hope the person coming doesn't want you, as I would love to massage you and help you feel better."

Oh why couldn't Jill take him home!

All the time that Jill worked on Buddy's father, Buddy strained against his rope to get closer to her. When the other lady arrived to meet him and see if she liked him, he had almost managed to reach Jill.

The new lady was loud and rough, and Buddy did not want to go home with her. Buddy shook his head up and down while she rode him; he was not happy at all. Luckily, this lady did not want Buddy; she thought he was naughty. Buddy was relieved.

Jill worked on Buddy and found that he was very sore indeed; his feet were out of balance and his saddle wasn't fitting him.

He also didn't like wearing the bit, as it banged the roof of his mouth and pressed on his tongue and against his teeth. No wonder he shook his head up and down when he was ridden and people didn't want to ride him.

Jill released his tension and massaged his muscles. Buddy felt fantastic. He closed his eyes and relaxed as she worked on him, and whenever he could reach, he licked her from head to toe.

Jill kept whispering to him, "You are a beautiful and sensitive horse, and you can do anything you want to do. I wish I could take you home."

Buddy wished she could take him home too.

CHAPTER SIX

Jill told Ginny what she had found. She showed her how Buddy's feet were out of balance, how the saddle didn't fit and what the bridle and bit were doing to his head and mouth. Ginny was amazed and agreed to work with Jill to correct these things.

Poor Buddy, he had tried so hard even though he was very unhappy and uncomfortable.

Over time Buddy's feet were balanced, his saddle was changed to one that fitted, and the bridle and bit were changed to be more comfortable. He loved his massages from Jill, but he was still so worried. The people who came to ride him were not like Jill.

One day a young woman called Kayla came to see Buddy, and she fell in love with Buddy as soon as she saw him. She was taller than Jill and rode Buddy well, and Ginny thought that she would give Buddy a great and loving home.

Buddy liked Kayla but not as much as Jill, and he was scared to leave his mother and father and Ginny and go to his new home with Kayla.

He neighed as he left the farm that had been his home for so long, and he shook in the horse trailer for the whole trip down the big mountain to Kayla's home by the sea.

The paddock was nice and shady, and he had a stable to escape the heat and flies and rain. There was an older horse there called Rex for company, and Kayla gave him lots of scratches, rubs and his favourite treats, carrots, to help him settle in.

All went well for the first few months. Kayla took great care of Buddy and had his feet balanced, and she rode him with the saddle and the bridle and bit that Jill had fitted. Ginny called every week to check how they were doing. But Buddy still missed Jill's massages.

Kayla changed her trainer, and this trainer, Mitchell, told Kayla that Buddy was beautiful and stunning but behind in his training for his age and needed to catch up.

After that the training became more difficult, and Buddy needed more time to work things out.

His muscles changed shape, and his saddle needed refitting, but Kayla and Mitchell didn't notice this and kept on asking him to do more difficult exercises.

Mitchell didn't like riding Buddy in the saddle that Jill had fitted, and he made Kayla buy another one that didn't fit Buddy at all.

And, to make it worse, Kayla changed farriers, and the new man was rough with Buddy and didn't keep his feet balanced.

Buddy became sorer and more scared every day until one day he started to shake his head up and down. Mitchell changed Buddy's bit and gave Kayla more difficult exercises for Buddy to stop him shaking his head, but he was more worried and scared every day.

If only they would understand me like Jill, he thought, and he longed for her every day.

Eventually, things became so bad that Mitchell told Kayla that Buddy was a dangerous horse to ride and that she should stop riding him immediately, sell him and buy another horse.

Kayla was very upset, and she phoned Ginny for help.

Ginny was devastated that things had got so bad and told Kayla she would buy Buddy back and find him his forever home.

CHAPTER SEVEN

Buddy was a very scared and confused horse now. He didn't understand what was happening to him, where he was going and what he had done wrong. He only knew that he wasn't happy and wanted to go home to his mother and father and Ginny.

When Ginny arrived to pick him up, he was so pleased to see her he neighed and galloped over to her and licked her from head to toe.

Ginny looked at his feet, which were not balanced, and at the marks on his body from the badly fitting saddle and in his mouth from the wrong bit. She was angry at Mitchell the trainer and sad for Kayla and Buddy that they had not been able to be happy together.

Ginny took Buddy home and started to work with him to regain his confidence. She was determined to find him a suitable owner who would give him his forever home.

She remembered how much Buddy had liked Jill and that Jill would be able to give him the best home but had not been able to afford to buy him.

Maybe things had changed for Jill and she would be able to buy him?

Ginny talked to Jill, and she was overjoyed to hear that Ginny wanted her to take Buddy, as long as he remained with her forever and was not sold to anyone else.

Ginny warned Jill that Buddy was not the horse that she remembered, and he was very frightened, particularly of men. So much so that he would only permit women to handle him. Jill agreed to come and visit, and she came in a few days.

When Jill arrived at the farm, Ginny met her at the barn door. "I am so pleased to see you, and I know someone else who will be overjoyed to see you too," she said.

Meanwhile, in the barn, Buddy was waiting in the corner of the stable, dreading who would walk through the door, when he heard a voice that he remembered from the past.

Could it be Jill, after all this time? he thought.

As Ginny and Jill walked closer to him, he caught Jill's scent, and he knew she had finally come to see him.

He rushed to the stable door, ears pricked, eyes bright.

It was Jill! Oh joy!

Jill looked at Buddy and saw the joy in his eyes and the worry lines on his face and the signs of neglect and ill treatment on his body, and she wanted to run to him and throw her arms around his neck.

But Jill knew that although he was pleased to see her, he might still be scared at the show of her feelings in a sudden rush.

So she held out her hand for him to sniff her palm, and she spoke quietly to him at almost a whisper. "Hello, my beautiful boy, I see you remember me. I have never forgotten you."

Buddy sniffed her fingers and then licked her from head to toe until she was sopping wet. Jill laughed as he licked her tears of joy away from her face.

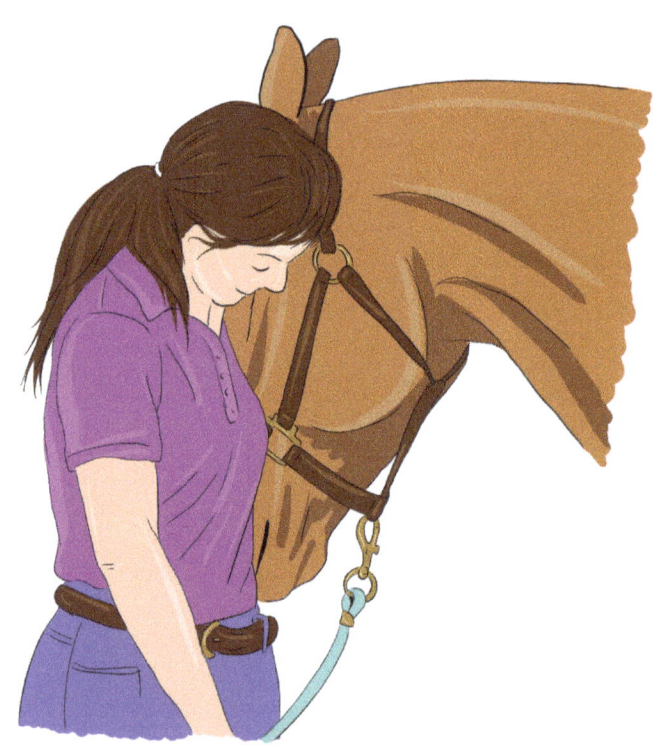

CHAPTER EIGHT

Jill took Buddy to his new forever home and introduced him to the rest of her herd.

Gus the bossy bay, Birdie the sensitive grey, Barney and Peep, who were retired racehorses, and George the tough pony. George was to be Buddy's paddock mate while he settled in to life with Jill.

At first Buddy was worried that he would have to share Jill with the others, but he soon realised that she had time and love for all of them.

Under Jill's care he slowly regained his confidence and strength. She massaged him and spent many hours with him in his paddock just talking to him and scratching him, which he loved.

He grew more confident day by day, and he started to run and play with George and soon felt brave enough to talk to the other horses over the fence.

Jill's farrier, Darrell, came to balance his feet, and Buddy was afraid and hid behind Jill, but Darrell was a kind man who deeply loved horses, and he could see that Buddy was scared. He approached Buddy slowly, holding out his hand, and said, "What a beautiful horse you are, Buddy. I want to help you and care for your feet and make you feel good."

Buddy could see that he was different from other men and more like Jill, and he blew deeply through his nostrils and stretched out his neck to smell Darrell's hand.

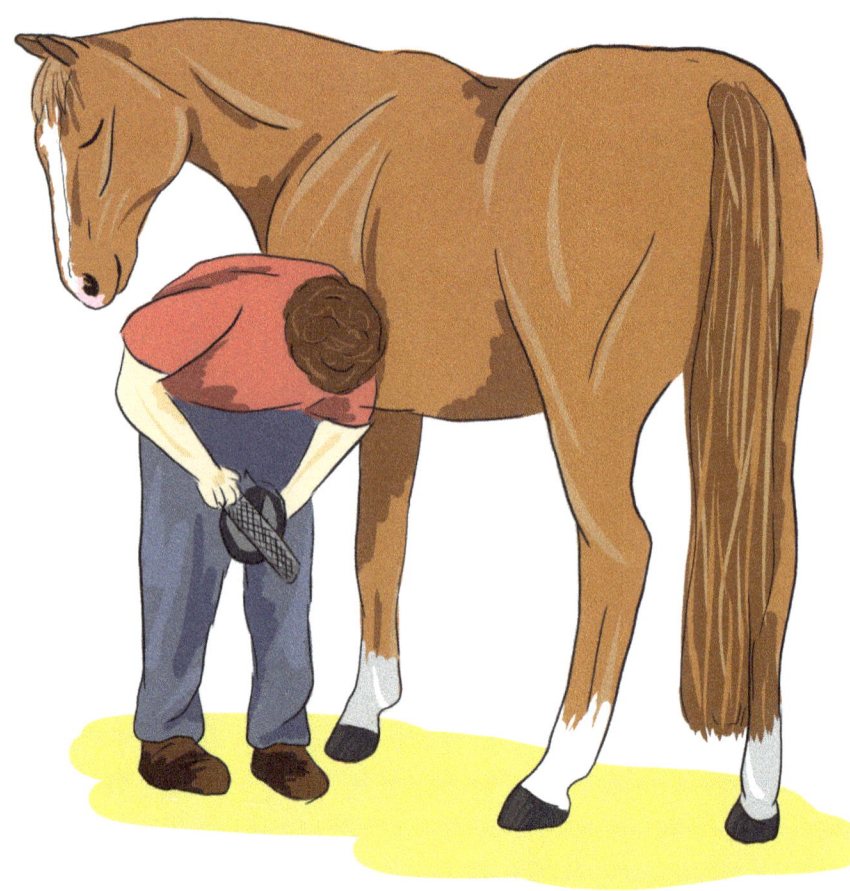

He smelt good, and Buddy took a lick of his hand, and he tasted good too! Maybe he was not going to hurt him.

Darrell handled Buddy's legs gently and balanced his feet while all the time Buddy licked him from head to toe and made him very wet!

Buddy was very happy that he had found his forever home with Jill, and now he could stop being so scared and start to help others with his big heart, and he went on to help many people, especially Jill through her struggles in life.

But that is another story.

Buddy

www.ingramcontent.com/pod-product-compliance
Lightning Source LLC
Chambersburg PA
CBHW040555010526
44110CB00054B/2725